READY FOR ANYTHING!
TRAINING YOUR BRAIN FOR EXPERT ESPIONAGE

by Heidi E. Y. Stemple

with Tony and Jonna Mendez
Consultants

Scholastic Inc.
New York • Toronto • London • Auckland • Sydney
Mexico City • New Delhi • Hong Kong • Buenos Aires

ISBN 0-439-90504-4
Copyright © 2006 by Scholastic Inc.

Designer: Aruna Goldstein
Illustrations: James W. Elston
Comic Strip Illustrations: Yancey Labat

Photos: Page 14: Time & Life Pictures/Getty Images. Page 23: International Spy Museum.
Page 29: International Spy Museum. Page 31: (author photo) David W. Stemple.

For information regarding permission, write to Scholastic Inc., Attention:
Permissions Department, 557 Broadway, New York, NY 10012.
SCHOLASTIC, THE ULTIMATE SPY CLUB, and associated logos are
trademarks and/or registered trademarks of Scholastic Inc.

12 11 10 9 8 7 6 5 4 3 2 1   6 7 8 9 10 11/0

Printed in the U.S.A.

First printing, November 2006

Table of Contents

If you look at a magazine and only see articles, it's time to get a spy's view of things! With some creativity and a little brainstorming, that magazine is a new way to collect information, pass info to co-spies, hide your true identity, and more!

When spies reach an obstacle, they need to find a clever way around it. Some spies have fancy gadgets to help, but it's a spy's ability to think on his feet and see things differently that really matters. Your best gadget? It's something you always have with you—your brain! A spy is more likely to use brains than muscles, so read on—it's time to get

ready! With your latest **Ultimate Spy Club** handbook and spy kit, you'll learn about...

Memory Games

Spies take time to train their brains so they're always ready to observe and remember important info. You'll learn how to play a game that real spies use to keep their memories sharp.

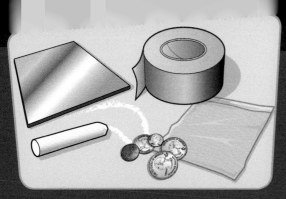

Everyday Objects

You'll learn how to use objects from around your house for all sorts of spying. And the best part? There's never anything suspicious about *these* spy gadgets.

Modifications

Sometimes it's important to know how to change or modify ordinary objects for your spy purposes. You'll see some items real spies have changed and make some modifications of your own. You'll even learn how to make your own spy jacket!

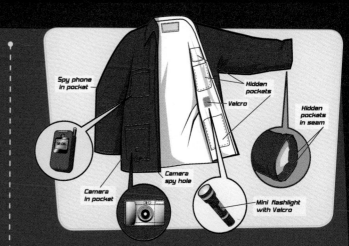

Spy phone in pocket

Hidden pockets

Velcro

Hidden pockets in seam

Camera in pocket

Camera spy hole

Mini flashlight with Velcro

And more!

Be sure to visit the
Ultimate Spy Club online at:
www.scholastic.com/ultimatespy

This month's secret password is:
getready

What's in Your Spy Kit?

can look like you're just talking on your phone or typing a text message—when you're really gathering important info!

Spy Phone

Your spy phone *looks* like an ordinary cell phone, but flip up the keypad and inside is a hidden notepad for all your observations and secret information. The antenna is actually a pen, and the light inside means you can do your spying anytime— day or night! A spy always needs to collect information, and with your spy phone, you'll always be ready!

Your spy phone can also help you keep your cool while spying, because it makes a great **cover**. You

3:05 pm - suspect left the building

12:05

MISSION #1:
GETTING READY

When you're a spy, there's no telling when you'll need to spring into action. That's why you need to make sure you're ready for anything that might come along. That means you've got to exercise your brain and plan ahead. Spies have to be able to stay alert, observe what's going on around them, and remember what they see.

Being ready also means making sure you have whatever gadgets and equipment you might need for your mission, scoping out the scene ahead of time, and having a cover story prepared. So get ready for some spy training. Then you'll always be ready, no matter what your mission is!

Here are some important things to keep in mind so you're always ready for an unexpected mission:

⇨ **Keep your eyes open**.
A spy is always watching. You need to stay aware of what's going on around you.

⇨ **Keep your ears open**.
Paying attention to what people are saying around you is another great way to get important information. And if you look busy, people often forget you can hear what they're saying.

⇨ **Exercise your memory**.
Being a spy means keeping your memory sharp. There are games and exercises you can do to give your memory a workout so it's always ready when you need it.

⇨ **Record information**. Carry around pencil and paper so you always have somewhere to store info and ideas that you might not be able to remember. (Your spy phone makes this easy!)

⇨ **Look natural**. Practice looking natural while you do your spying. It's important to be able to blend in and not look suspicious!

POP Culture

James Bond's gadget man, Q, made some of the fanciest gadgets around, like a missile-launching car and a watch with a laser-beam cutter. But even with all these gadgets, Bond still has to think quickly. In one of his adventures he grabs a scarf and wraps it around his head as a quick-change disguise. In another, he uses medical equipment in his hospital room to help him escape.

All Set for Spying

If you're working with a spy group, you need to be extra prepared! You'll need to make plans with your co-spies before setting out on any mission to make sure everybody's on the same page.

Here are a few things for your group to decide on before setting out on a mission:

Headquarters. Agree on a **secure** location to meet at.

Signals. It's important to have a way to alert your fellow spies. Come up with signals for different situations— a danger signal, a signal to call a meeting, and a signal for when info is ready to be picked up. Then make sure to keep your eyes open for the signs!

Codes. Codes are a great way to safely communicate with fellow spies. Make up a code with your friends and make sure everybody knows how to use it.

Dead drop locations. If you'll need to leave communications for your co-spies to pick up, make sure you decide where you're going to **dead drop** it. Decide on a signal to alert your co-spies when the info's ready to be picked up.

Decide these things together and be sure to record them in a spy log or in your spy phone. That way you'll always have the info when you need it.

Kim's Game

What do you do if you come across some important info but don't have any paper? Or what if the info's so secret it isn't safe to write it down? That's when having a strong memory comes in handy.

Kipling's Kim

Kim is a book by Rudyard Kipling (who also wrote *The Jungle Book*). It tells the story of a young orphan boy in India who becomes friends with a spy. The spy sees potential in Kim and begins training him in **espionage**. Since memory is very important to spying, Kim is challenged to the Jewel Game by another boy.

The Game

In the Jewel Game, players are shown a tray of jewels. When one minute has passed, the tray is covered, and the person who remembers the most jewels wins. At first, Kim loses the game. In fact, he can only remember a few jewels. Then Kim practices until he can not only name all the jewels, but describe each one, too. This game is now called "Kim's Game," and it's played by many people, including the Girl and Boy Scouts. It's even used by real spies to help make their memories supersharp.

Playing Kim's Game

Try playing Kim's Game with your friends or by yourself. It'll strengthen your memory and your spying.

You Need:

- ✓ Small objects (about 20)
- ✓ Timer
- ✓ Tray
- ✓ Cloth
- ✓ Paper and pencils

How to Play:

- Place the objects on the tray and cover them with the cloth.
- Uncover the tray and set the timer for one minute.
- When the minute is over, cover the tray again and have each player write down all of the objects they can remember.
- The player who remembers the most objects wins!

For a variation on the game: After the minute has passed and the tray is covered up again, have someone remove an object. Then uncover the tray and see who can figure out which object is missing the fastest.

SPY TIP:

Here are some tricks to help you play Kim's Game:

Think of the objects in groups. If there are four kitchen items, think of them as a set.

Think of the objects in a room in your house. When you need to recall them, think of the room and where each item is. What objects were on the desk you made up in your mind?

Think of the first letter of each object and group them together that way: button, battery, baseball, bobby pin.

Can you think of other tricks to help you remember?

Recon Ready

Spies need to be able to blend into their surroundings and not look suspicious. This means that acting can play a big role in spying. It also means that doing research and being prepared are really important. If you need to blend in somewhere, it's a good idea to do **reconnaissance**, or **recon**, to gather information.

Take a trip to the area where you plan to spy and have a look around. Here are some things for you to pay attention to while you're on your reconnaissance mission:

⇨ In order to blend in, will you need to dress a certain way?

⇨ How are people in the area acting? Pay attention to where people are and who they're talking to.

⇨ If there's a risk of getting caught, will you need a cover story to explain why you're there?

⇨ What items should you make sure to have with you?

⇨ Where is the best place to stand or sit?

⇨ Is there a spot to hide in or a way to exit quickly if you need to?

⇨ Who are you likely to see? Will they get in the way, or help you with your cover?

With your recon notes ready, you'll be all set for your spy mission!

POP Culture

In the movie *National Treasure*, the heroes know it isn't safe for them to get the info they need to crack a code. Instead, they hire a young boy to get the info for them.

Cell Phone Subterfuge

Your spy phone is a great way to blend in with your surroundings. Since cell phones are everywhere, no one will notice a kid sitting and talking, text messaging, or playing a game on their cell phone. That means your spy phone can make a great cover for your spying. If you act like you're concentrating on your phone, no one will suspect you're actually listening and observing.

You're No Phone-y

Do some recon beforehand to get comfortable with the role you'll be playing—a kid talking on their cell phone. Spend some time watching other people on their cell phones.

⇨ How do they act while they're talking? Do they sit still? Do they move around?

⇨ Where do people carry their phones when they're not using them?

⇨ What do people do with their hands when they're talking?

⇨ Where do people look while they're talking? Do they look straight ahead? At the ground?

⇨ How do people look when they're text messaging? How about when they're playing games on their phone?

SIR ROBERT BADEN-POWELL

Be prepared! It's the motto of the Boy Scouts. But what do Scouts and spies have in common? The scouting movement was started by one of the best British spies in history!

Robert Baden-Powell was an officer in the British army. He was very good at his job and began spying in enemy territory. Then in 1899, Baden-Powell wrote a book called *Aids to Scouting*. He meant it as a military textbook, but it was soon being used to teach young boys woodworking and outdoor skills. Baden-Powell thought this was a great idea and set up a camp for boys. That was the beginning of the Boy Scouts.

Robert Baden-Powell was always prepared to blend in. But he didn't wear a funny mustache and a fake nose. This resourceful spy disguised himself as a lepidopterist (someone who collects and studies butterflies) in the Balkan Islands, where war was about to break

FIELD GUNS

FORTRESS GUNS

OUTLINE OF THE FORTRESS

out. He carried a butterfly net and a sketchbook, and everyone left him alone, thinking he was minding his own business. He drew large pictures of butterflies that contained very detailed sketches of the Austrian fortifications being made for guns and ammunition for the coming war.

On another spy mission, Baden-Powell disguised himself as a hunter and hid his sketchbook in his hunting bag. With his gun and hunting dog by his side, the soldiers building foundations for war guns barely even noticed him, and he was once again able to roam the countryside sketching where enemy guns would be.

Robert Baden-Powell didn't have a lot of fancy spy gadgets, but he knew the importance of pencil and paper. Even more than that, he knew the importance of being prepared and thinking creatively.

A Clever Cover

Sometimes it's not enough to look natural. Even if you blend in, it's possible that an enemy spy might question you. A spy needs to be able to think quickly, but it's better to have a story ready beforehand. That way you'll be ready and can sound as natural as possible.

SPY HISTORY uNcoVEREd

In 1979, during the Iranian Hostage Crisis, CIA officer Tony Mendez used a clever cover to rescue six American diplomats who were hiding in Iran. He and the six diplomats posed as members of a Hollywood movie production company scouting locations in Iran for a film they were making. The cover story worked and all six diplomats were returned home safely.

Here are some important things to think about before heading out on a mission:

- If you're pretending to speak on your spy phone, be ready to say who you're talking to in case someone asks.

- Sometimes you have to get into a tricky spot to do surveillance or evidence gathering. If someone asks why you're there, how will you explain it?

- What will you say if you get caught passing intelligence to a fellow spy?

SPY TIP:

Keep your cover story simple. It's easier to remember a cover story if it doesn't involve lots of detail. If someone asks who's on the phone, saying "my mom" is a lot easier and more believable than diving into a long story about your conversation.

MISSION #2: EVERYDAY ESPIONAGE

One great way to stay ready for anything is to know how to use the everyday things around you for spying. Thanks to your spy phone, you'll always be ready with pen and paper. But what do you do when you need to find your way around, read something small, or hear an important conversation?

There are a ton of everyday items that can help. Keep some of these things around in your spy kit and then you'll have what you need when the moment strikes. And the best thing about these gadgets? There's nothing suspicious about 'em!

These are only a few of the things that can come in handy. Do some brainstorming and see what other ideas you can dream up.

Super simple Spy Kit

There isn't always time to run off and collect your spy gear. That's why most spies carry some tools with them all the time. Having a spy kit with you keeps you prepared. And if you fill your kit with items that you find around the house, you won't look suspicious!

Here are 5 great items with a ton of different spy uses that you could include in your spy kit. Remember, anything you put in your kit should be small enough to carry in your pocket or backpack and should have multiple uses so you don't waste space!

Plastic Bags

A sealable plastic bag is a great everyday item to put in your spy kit. In fact, it can hold the other items!

⇨ If you're leaving an important note at an outside dead drop, you can use a plastic bag to make sure that note stays safe and dry until it's picked up.

⇨ Sealable bags are watertight. That means they can keep important equipment and communications dry while you go about your mission.

⇨ If there's important evidence you need to collect, a sealable plastic bag will help you keep it safe until you're ready to **analyze** it later.

A plastic grocery bag is also very useful. It crinkles up small and can do a lot!

⇨ Spies can change their appearance quickly by taking off a jacket, hat, or extra shirt and slipping them into a grocery bag.

One mark can mean "the coast is clear," and two can mean "wait for my signal."

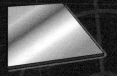 Leave arrows on the sidewalk as directions to a fellow spy.

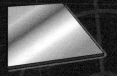 Use chalk marks as a signal to let your fellow spies know what spots have been checked and are secure or empty.

Mirror

A small mirror can help out in all kinds of ways.

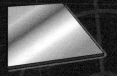 Mirror-image codes (a message written backward) can be written and decoded using a mirror.

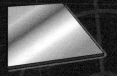 Slip a bag over your feet to keep from leaving footprints, or over your hand so you don't leave fingerprints.

Chalk

A piece of chalk is another smart item to have in your spy kit. It's small and washes off easily, which makes it perfect for covering up your tracks.

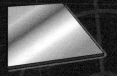 Make up an easy code and leave chalk marks on the sidewalk or a mailbox.

19

Attach a mirror to the pages of a book or magazine. While pretending to read, you can watch what's going on behind you!

Catch light in a mirror to signal another spy or catch someone's attention.

Duct Tape

Duct tape—the strong, thick, gray tape—is another useful item.

Keep a note or secret document out of sight by taping it inside the cuff of your jeans or up your sleeve.

Use a loop of tape to make a sneaky dead drop underneath a table or desk.

⇨ Cover the bottoms of your shoes to keep from leaving footprints.

⇨ Use the superstrong tape to fix anything that comes apart while you're on your mission.

⇨ Twist the duct tape to quickly make some strong rope.

Money

Money can be an important tool as well. Make sure you always have enough to make a phone call. Then learn how to put those coins to good use.

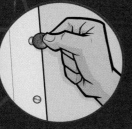

⇨ A coin can be used as a screwdriver or a prying tool.

⇨ Coins can be used to signal fellow spies. You could leave a penny behind a tree or under a doormat to tell your co-spies that a meeting will be held at spy headquarters. A nickel could mean the meeting is canceled.

⇨ Dropping some coins on the ground is a great way to distract people and buy some time.

21

Listening In

It's always important to keep your ears open, but sometimes it's hard to hear the things you need to. That's why spies often use fancy listening equipment or **bugs**. But what about when you don't have fancy gadgets? Spies can always find creative ways to do their spying.

Paper

Try rolling a piece of paper into a cone. Place the wide end of the cone up against a wall or door and put the narrow end up to your ear. The cone will amplify sound enough for you to hear things you might otherwise miss. Experiment to see where this works best, and try making the cone with different sizes of paper. Does a bigger cone make the sound louder?

SPY TIP:

Even when spying, it's important to respect other people's privacy. Even the U.S. government needs a judge's permission before they can listen in on a conversation.

Cup

A cup can help you hear through doors and walls too. Put the open side of a cup up against a wall. Then place your ear against the bottom of the cup.

Tricky Technology

Walkie-talkies can also be used as listening devices. Try taping down the speaking button on one walkie-talkie and hiding it in a room. Then take the other walkie-talkie with you. Test it out with a friend and see what you can hear.

REAL SPY GADGETS

Real life spies conceal microphones and bugs (listening devices) in all sorts of things including phones, lamps, jewelry, pens, and pagers. This fake tree stump is actually a listening device created by the CIA. It was placed in the woods near a Soviet military base and used to pick up secret radio transmissions.

Instant Intelligence

Passing **intelligence**, like a top secret note, can be tough. Sometimes you need a more creative way to get that info passed safely. Here are some everyday items that can help.

➭ **Film canister.** The black plastic canister that camera film comes in is watertight. It can help you conceal a message to leave at a dead drop and keep that message safe and dry. Or you can pretend you're giving your friend a roll of film and hand the note off directly.

➭ **Clothing.** A note hidden in a jacket pocket or tucked into a hatband can be passed by lending that piece of clothing to a friend.

➭ **Magazine.** A spy can conceal a secret document inside the pages of a book or magazine. Then it's simple to hand off that note or leave it to be picked up by a co-spy.

➭ **Pen.** Some pens can be taken apart and used to conceal a tightly rolled-up note. If you screw the top back on, no one will ever know that the pen you borrowed from a friend really contains secret information.

Seeing the Big Picture

Keeping your eyes open and being able to see what's going on are very important to espionage. Sometimes that means you'll need the help of a few tools.

Magnifying Mission

What if you've been given super small clues and secret info? You might need a magnifying glass or even a microscope. But if you don't have one, don't worry! A good spy always has a plan!

⇨ **Glasses.** Some reading glasses can also work as magnifying glasses. Just hold them over a tiny message and you're in the clear.

⇨ **Water.** A drop of water can magnify a message as well. Put a square of waxed paper on top of a page of small text. Then use an eyedropper to put a drop of water on the waxed paper, and see what a difference it makes.

⇨ **Paper clip.** Bend a paper clip into a small loop and dip it into a glass of water or bubble solution. The water it catches will work as a magnifying glass.

marble and place it at the corner of one sheet of paper. Roll the paper tightly around the marble to form a tube. The marble should be sticking halfway out of one end of the tube.

Make a plain tube with the second sheet of paper and try looking through each tube, one at a time. How much can you see with each?

Expand Your View

What if you need to see around a corner? Or scope out a big area while staying hidden? With this homemade gadget, you'll be able to see a whole lot—no matter how small a view you start out with. All you need are some black construction paper and a clear marble.

Cut a piece of black construction paper in half so you have two pieces that are about 9x6 inches each. Take a clear

Finding Your Way

Knowing where you are and how to get where you're going are very important. A compass is a great tool that will tell you which direction you're headed: north, south, east, or west. You may not always have a compass in your spy kit, but no worries. Here are two easy ways to make your own.

Magnet and Needle Compass

Rub an ordinary sewing needle across a magnet 50 to 60 times in one direction, or leave its tip on a magnet overnight. Stick the magnetized needle through a small piece of cork and float it in a cup of water. The tip will point north!

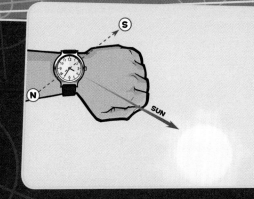

Wristwatch Compass

Point the hour hand of your watch in the direction of the sun. Then picture an imaginary line between the hour hand and the number 12. That imaginary line is pointing south. That means that the opposite direction is north!

SPY TIP:

How does a compass work? Earth is actually surrounded by a huge magnetic field with magnetic poles at the north and south. That means that Earth itself works like a magnet! A compass has a magnetized needle in it, which will always point north—toward the magnetic north pole of Earth.

Spy Jacket

One way to always be ready is to have everything needed for your mission on you and safely hidden away. How do you do that? How about with a special spy jacket you make yourself? Ask an adult for an old jacket you'd be allowed to change. Then ask for their help and get ready to add hidden pockets, gadgets, and more!

Hidden Pockets

Cut a square of fabric (make sure it's larger than the item you want to store). Ask an adult to help you sew three sides of the pocket onto the inside of your spy jacket, leaving the top open.

Velcro

Light weight items that you'll need quickly can be attached to the inside of your jacket with sticky Velcro tape. Simply stick one piece of Velcro into the inside of your jacket and stick the other side to the spy item itself.

Collar and Cuffs

Areas of a jacket that fold over—like its collar and sleeve cuffs—can be sewn shut to make extra hidden storage spots.

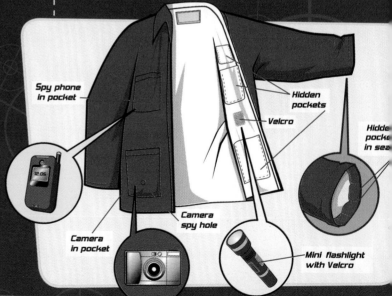

Spy phone in pocket

Hidden pockets

Velcro

Hidde pocke in sea

Camera spy hole

Camera in pocket

Mini flashlight with Velcro

REAL SPY GADGETS

These boots were designed by the British intelligence service for pilots during World War II. They had a small knife hidden in the bootstrap that could be used to cut off the top part of the boot. That left the pilot with normal-looking walking shoes so they could blend in once they landed in enemy territory.

Outside Pockets

Use your outside pockets for spy gadgets that are already disguised, like your spy phone. That way you can save the secret spaces inside for the gadgets that look more suspicious.

Cameras

If you plan to use a camera for a spy mission, you can keep the camera in a special pocket that will let you take pictures **covertly**. With an adult's permission, cut a hole in the pocket to the outside (just big enough to take pictures through). Then line the lens up with the hole and snap away. It'll look like you're just strolling along with your hand in your pocket, when you're really doing important **surveillance** work!

POP Culture

In *The Goonies*, Data, who wishes he were James Bond, wears a very cool jacket that conceals all the gadgets he made using everyday objects. Some of these gadgets include Data's "Pinchers of Peril" (mechanical toy teeth that grab onto a wall) and the cord for his "Slick Shoes" (sneakers that squirt oil).

Quick-Change Disguises

One quick and easy way to change your appearance is the **quick-change disguise**. It only requires a few extra pieces of clothing, and a little planning and quick thinking.

➪ **Layers**. Many people remember a person by the color of the shirt they're wearing. You can use this to your advantage by wearing two brightly-colored T-shirts, one on top of the other. When you need to change your identity and blend in, just remove the top T-shirt and stuff it in a backpack or shopping bag. Then when someone's looking for "the kid in the red shirt," you'll have quietly become "the kid in the yellow shirt."

➪ **Eyeglasses**. Eyeglasses are another great way to quickly change your appearance. Try using sunglasses, or a pair of old eyeglasses that you can remove the lenses from (with permission, of course).

➪ **Hats**. Use a hat for another quick and easy change.

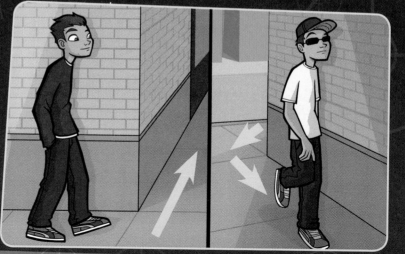

Mission Accomplished!

Now you know how to train your memory, use a ton of everyday items for top secret spying, and even make a few spy gadgets of your own. With your brain and your memory fine-tuned and more than a few tricks up your sleeve, you're ready for anything!

HEIDI E. Y. STEMPLE
Writer

Before jumping into the family business of writing, Heidi E. Y. Stemple worked in law enforcement and as a private investigator. Now she is the author of a dozen books for children including *One If By Land, A Massachusetts Number Book, Dear Mother, Dear Daughter,* and *Sleep, Black Bear, Sleep.* She lives in Massachusetts with her two daughters and one very crazy cat who is rumored to be a spy.

TONY AND JONNA MENDEZ
Consultants

Tony and Jonna spent their careers at the CIA. They worked overseas protecting American spies and the foreign assets working for the U.S. government. They were specialists in disguise and documents. Tony Mendez was named as one of the CIA's top spies in the last 50 years.

Glossary

Here are some spy words that you need to know:

Analyze – To study and figure out the importance of information or evidence

Bug – A miniature listening device that can transmit sound from one room to another

Conceal – Hide

Cover – A made-up story that a spy uses to blend in and keep their spying secret

Covert – Secret, undercover. Spying is a covert activity.

Dead Drop – A prearranged spot to pick up or drop off something left by or for another spy

Espionage – Spying to get information about the plans and activities of others

Intelligence – Information

Quick-Change Disguise – A disguise technique that involves quick and simple changes in appearance

Reconnaissance or **Recon**– An exploratory survey to gain information

Secure – Safe

Subterfuge – Deception. The act of pretending in order to gain something.

Surveillance – To watch someone or something